ALAN JACKSON

∽ PRECIOUS MEMORIES ∽

ISBN-13: 978-1-4234-1761-3

HAL•LEONARD®
CORPORATION
7777 W. BLUEMOUND RD. P.O. BOX 13819 MILWAUKEE, WI 53213

Visit Hal Leonard Online at
www.halleonard.com

BLESSED ASSURANCE

Lyrics by FANNY J. CROSBY
Music by PHOEBE PALMER KNAPP

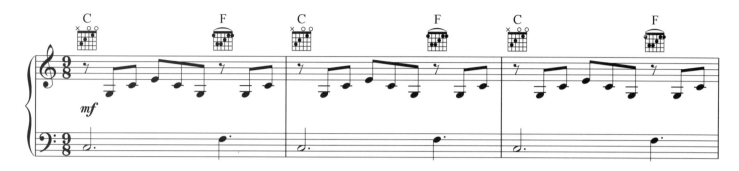

Bless - ed as - sur - rance, Je - sus is mine! _____ Oh, what a
mis - sion, per - fect de - light, _____ vi - sions of

fore - taste of glo - ry di - vine! _____ Heir of sal - va - tion, pur - chase of
rap - ture now burst on my sight. _____ An - gels de - scend - ing bring from a -

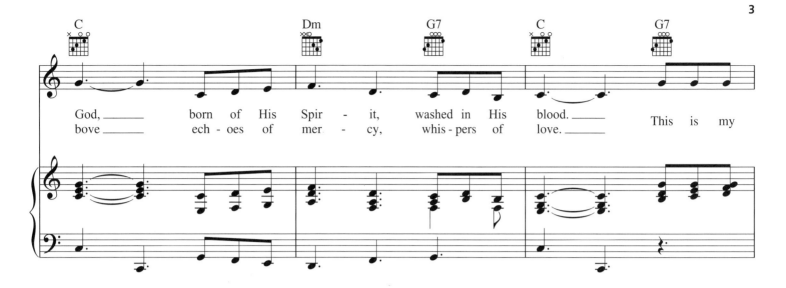

God, _____ born of His Spir - it, washed in His blood. _____
bove _____ ech - oes of mer - cy, whis - pers of love. _____ This is my

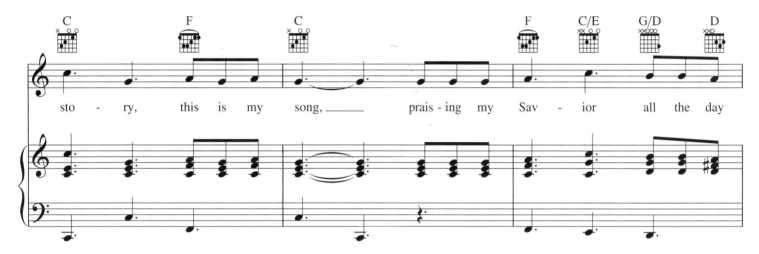

sto - ry, this is my song, _____ prais - ing my Sav - ior all the day

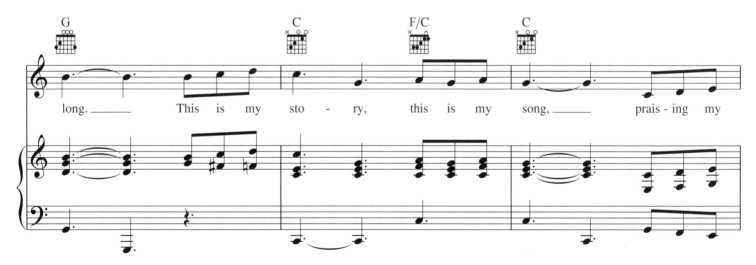

long. _____ This is my sto - ry, this is my song, _____ prais - ing my

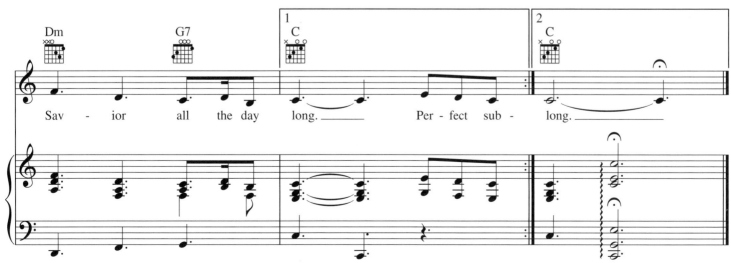

Sav - ior all the day long. _____ Per - fect sub - long. _____

I LOVE TO TELL THE STORY

Words by A. CATHERINE HANKEY
Music by WILLIAM G. FISCHER

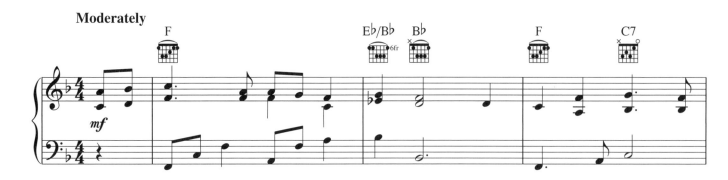

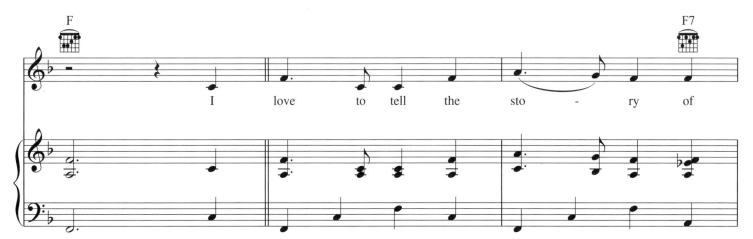

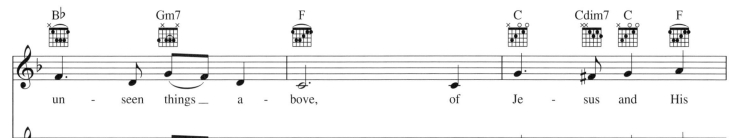

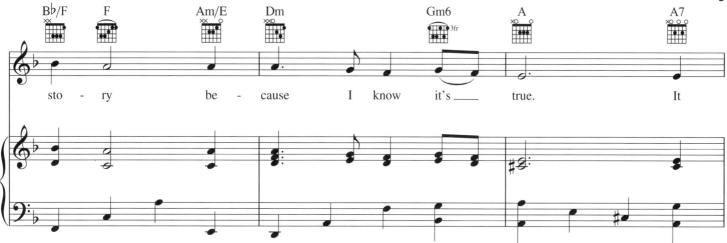

story be - cause I know it's _____ true. It

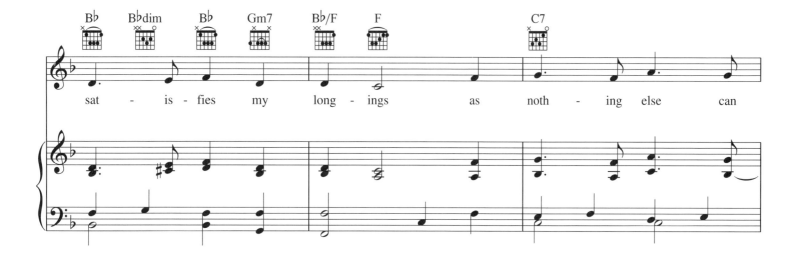

sat - is - fies my long - ings as noth - ing else can

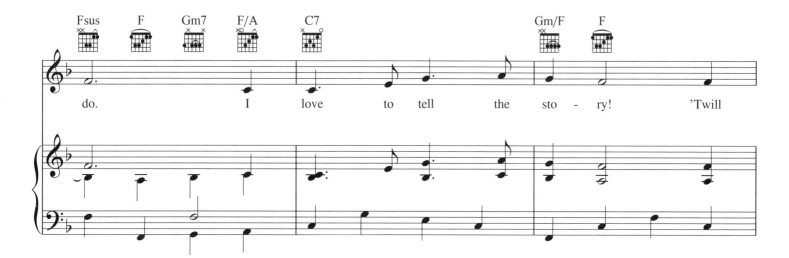

do. I love to tell the sto - ry! 'Twill

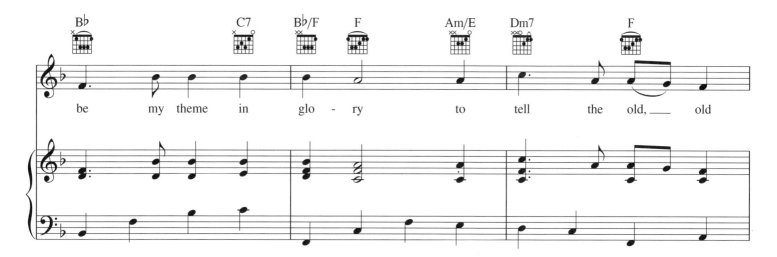

be my theme in glo - ry to tell the old, _____ old

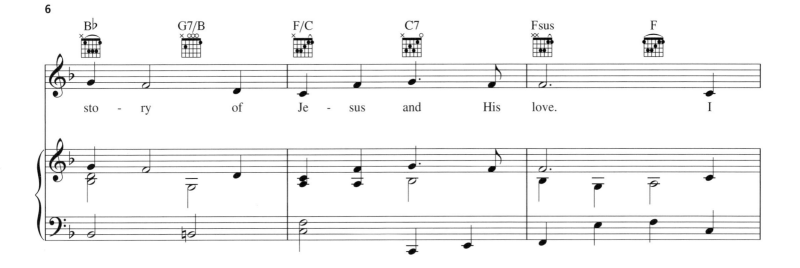

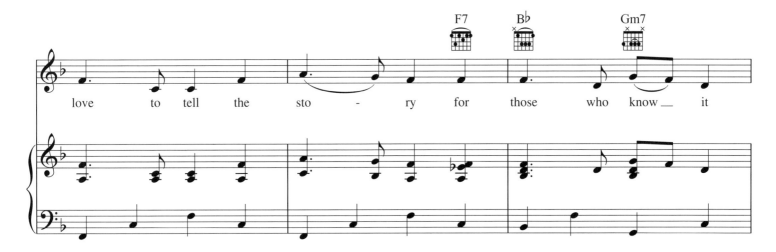

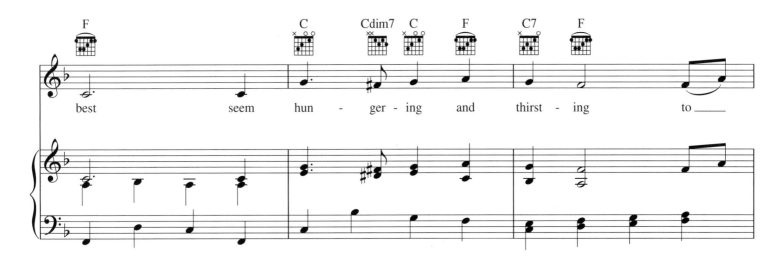

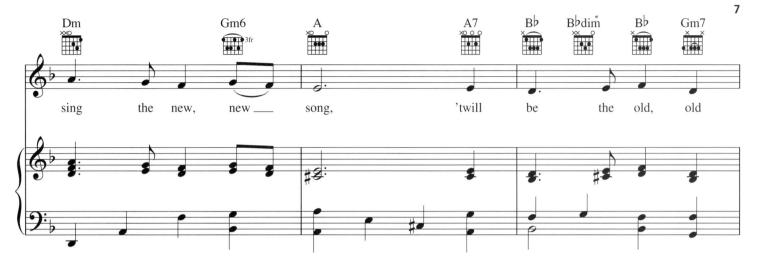

sing the new, new ___ song, 'twill be the old, old

sto - ry that I have loved so long. I

love to tell the sto - ry! 'Twill be my theme in glo - ry to

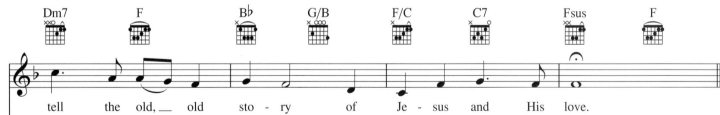

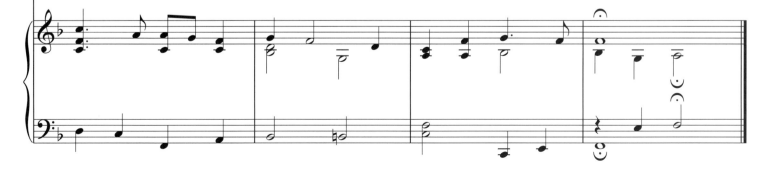

tell the old, ___ old sto - ry of Je - sus and His love.

WHEN WE ALL GET TO HEAVEN

Words by ELIZA E. HEWITT
Music by EMILY D. WILSON

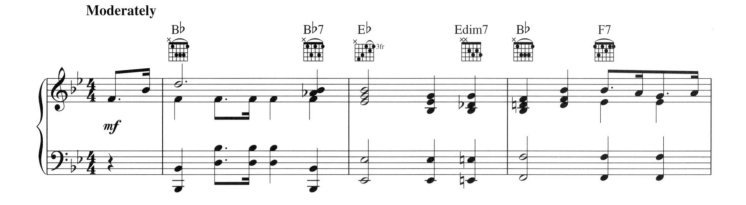

1. Sing the won-drous love ___ of ___ Je - sus;
2. On - ward to the prize ___ be - fore us!

Sing His mer - cy ___ and His grace. In the man - sions,
Soon His beau - ty ___ we'll be - hold. Soon the pearl - y

'TIS SO SWEET TO TRUST IN JESUS

Words by LOUISA M.R. STEAD
Music by WILLIAM J. KIRKPATRICK

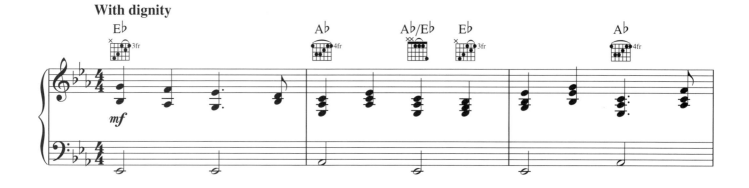

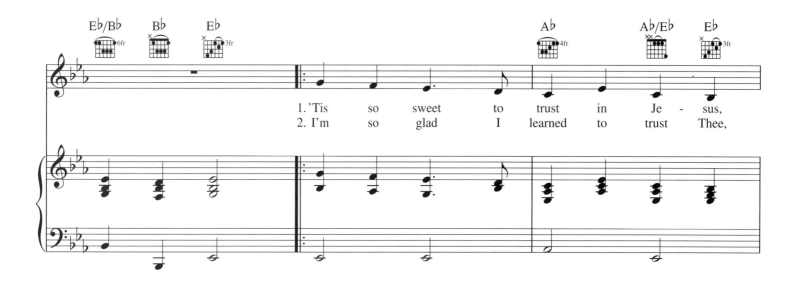

1. 'Tis so sweet to trust in Je-sus,
2. I'm so glad I learned to trust Thee,

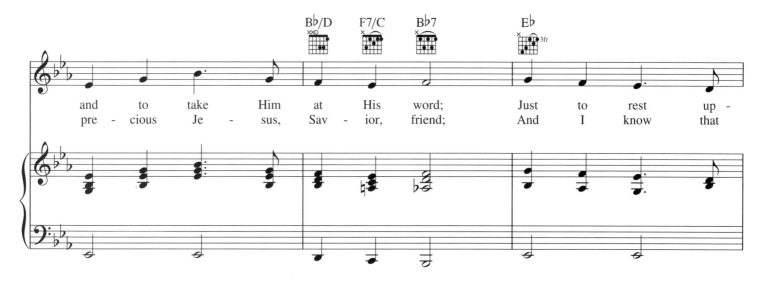

and to take Him at His word; Just to rest up-
pre-cious Je-sus, Sav-ior, friend; And I know that

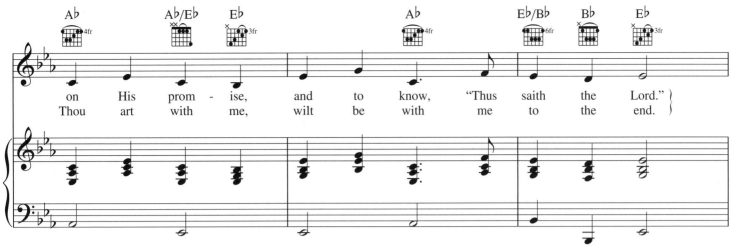

on His prom - ise, and to know, "Thus saith the Lord."
Thou art with me, and wilt to be with me to the end.

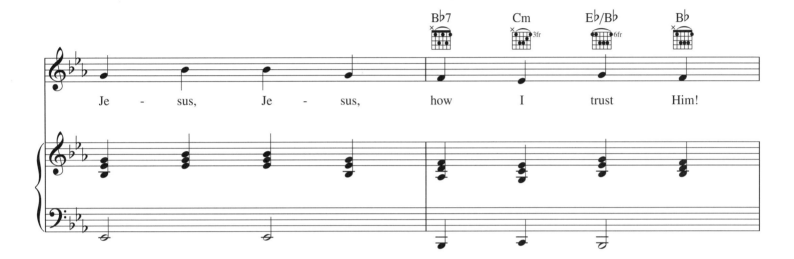

Je - sus, Je - sus, how I trust Him!

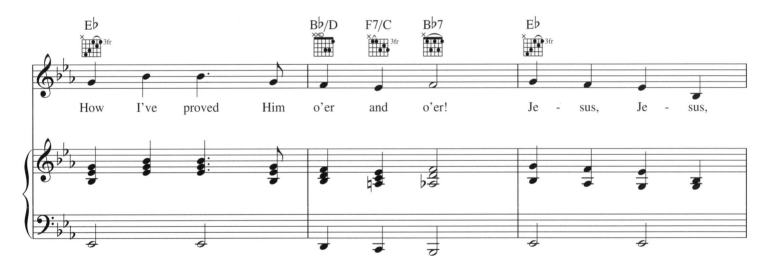

How I've proved Him o'er and o'er! Je - sus, Je - sus,

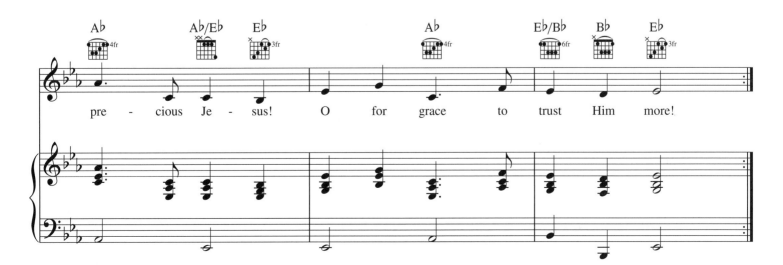

pre - cious Je - sus! O for grace to trust Him more!

SOFTLY AND TENDERLY

Words and Music by
WILL L. THOMPSON

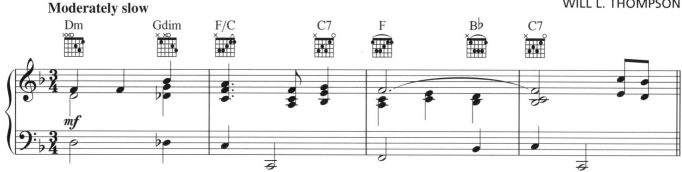

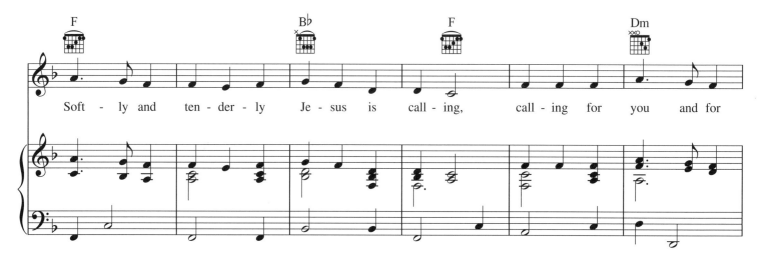

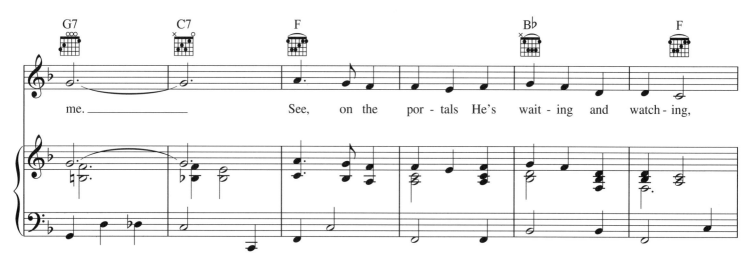

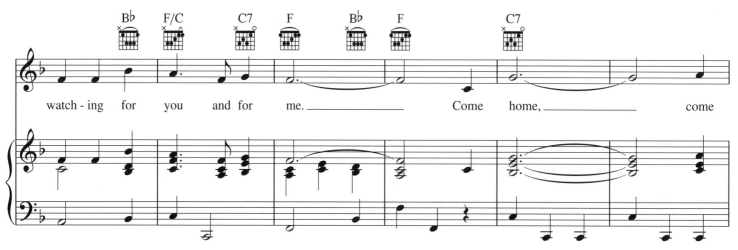

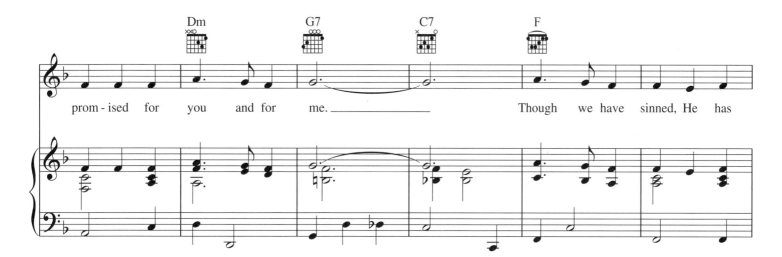

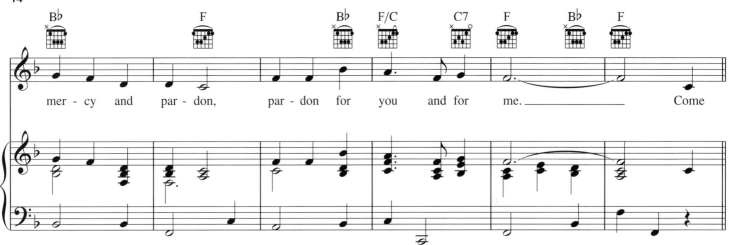

mer-cy and par-don, par-don for you and for me. _____ Come

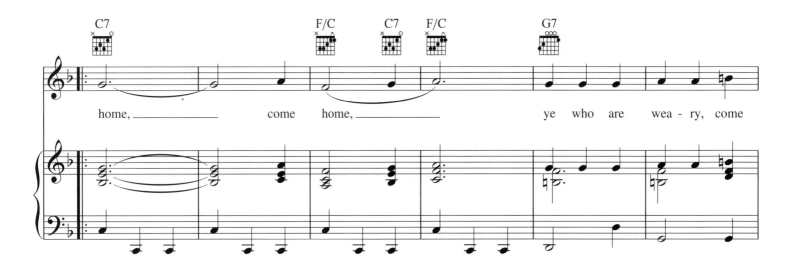

home, _____ come home, _____ ye who are wea-ry, come

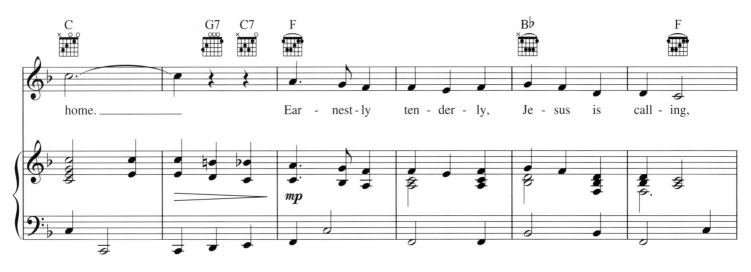

home. _____ Ear-nest-ly ten-der-ly, Je-sus is call-ing,

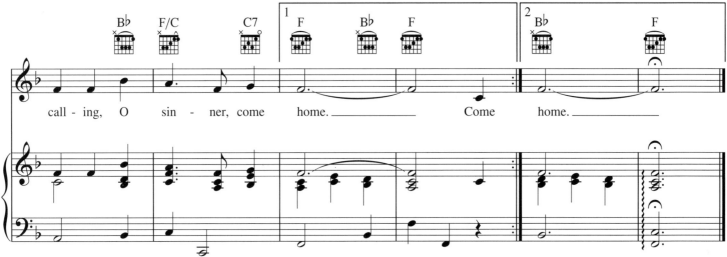

call-ing, O sin-ner, come home. _____ Come home. _____

IN THE GARDEN

Words and Music by
C. AUSTIN MILES

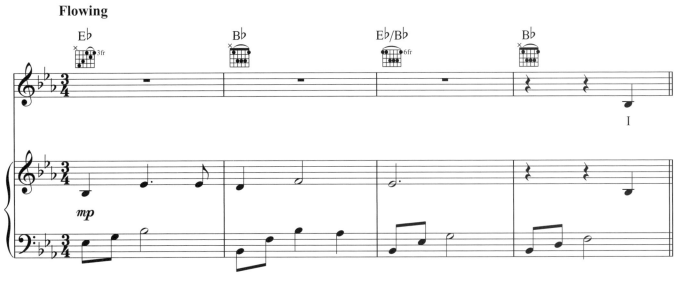

come to the gar - den a - lone, _____ while the
stay in the gar - den with Him, _____ though the

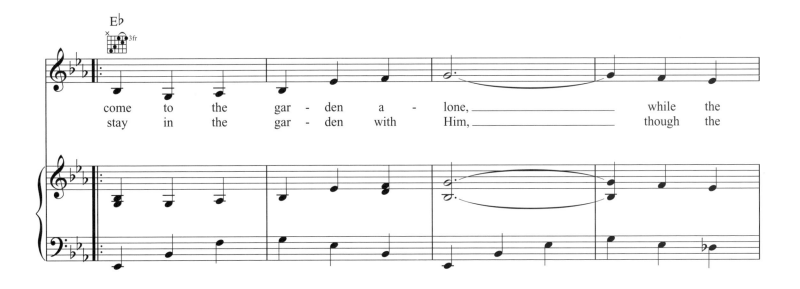

dew is still on the ros - es; and the
night a - round me is fall - ing; but He

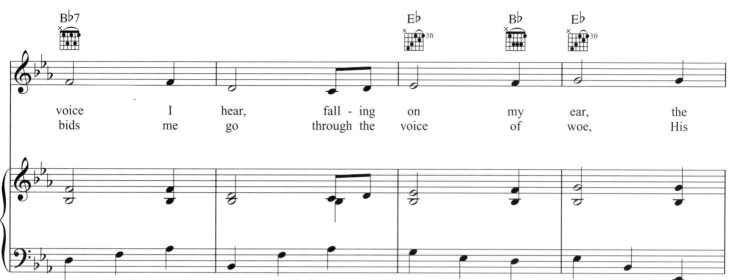

voice   I   hear,   fall - ing   on   my   ear,   the
bids   me   go   through the   voice   of   woe,   His

Son   of   God   dis - clos   -   es.   } And   He
voice   to   me   is   call   -   ing.

walks   with   me   and   He   talks   with   me,   and   He

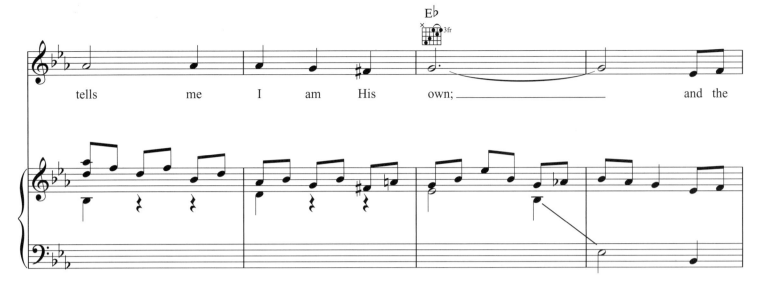

tells me I am His own; _____ and the

joy we share as we tar - ry there, none oth - er has

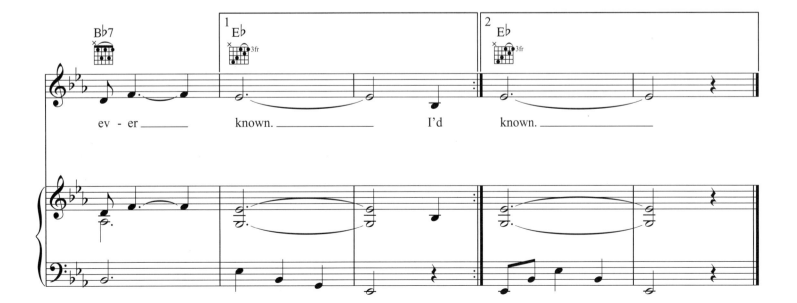

ev - er _____ known. _____ I'd known. _____

ARE YOU WASHED IN THE BLOOD?

Words and Music by
ELISHA A. HOFFMAN

Moderately

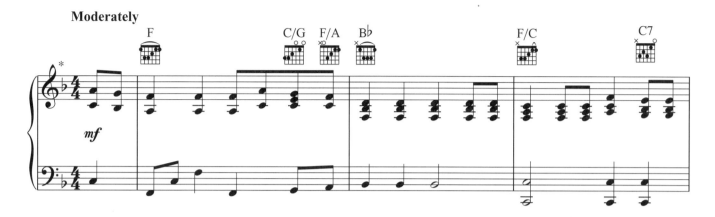

1. Have you been to Je-sus for the cleans-ing pow'r? Are you
2. side the gar-ments that are stained with sin, and be

washed in the blood of the Lamb? Are you full-y trust-ing in His
washed in the blood of the Lamb; There's a foun-tain flow-ing for the

Recorded a half step higher.

I'LL FLY AWAY

Words and Music by
ALBERT E. BRUMLEY

Fast and lively

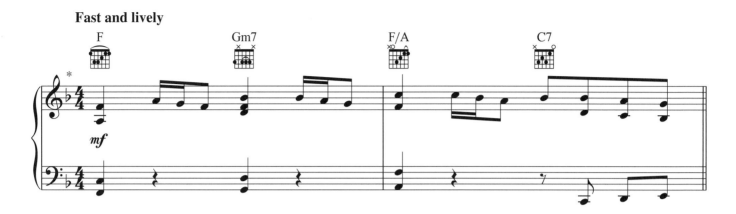

Some glad morn-ing when this life is o'er, ___
Instumental solo ad lib.
Just a few more wea-ry days and then, ___

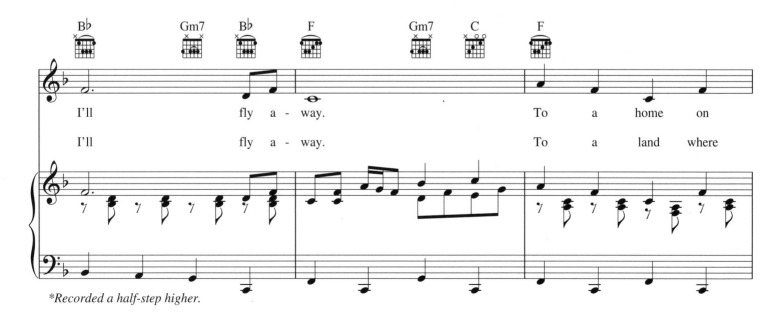

I'll fly a-way. To a home on
I'll fly a-way. To a land where

Recorded a half-step higher.

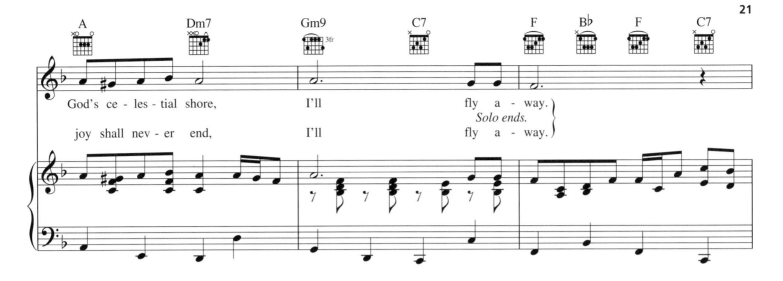

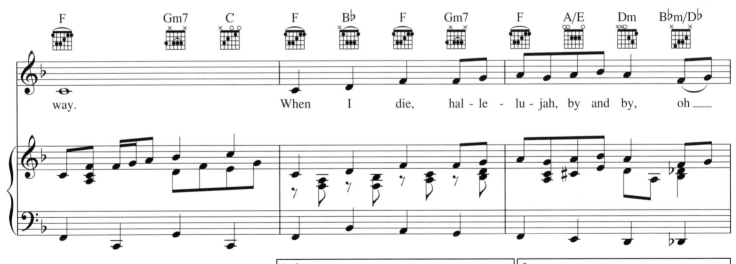

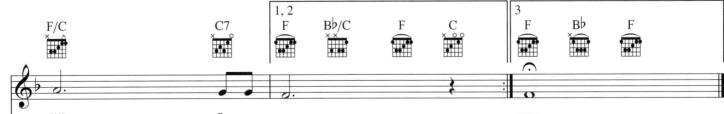

WHAT A FRIEND WE HAVE IN JESUS

Words by JOSEPH M. SCRIVEN
Music by CHARLES C. CONVERSE

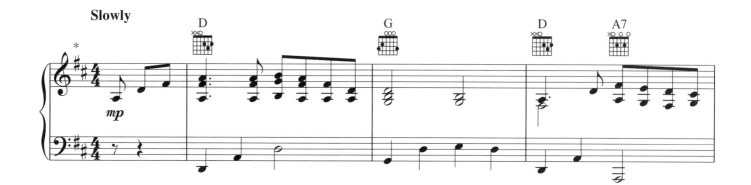

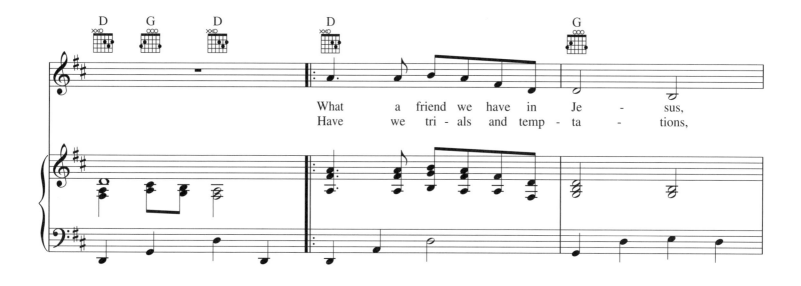

What a friend we have in Je - sus,
Have we tri - als and temp - ta - tions,

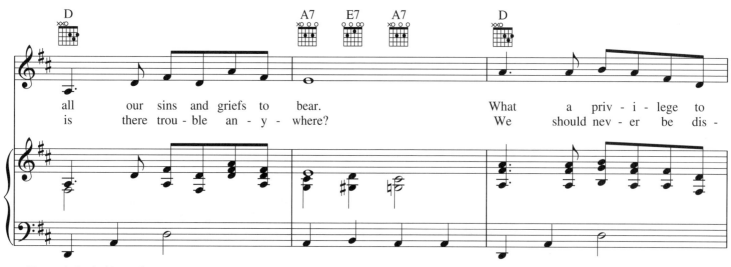

all our sins and griefs to bear.
is there trou - ble an - y - where?

What a priv - i - lege to
We should nev - er be dis -

*Recorded a half-step lower.

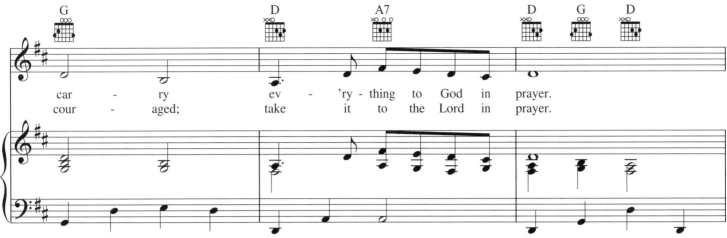

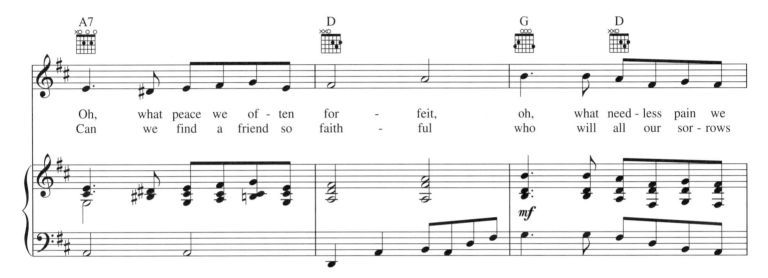

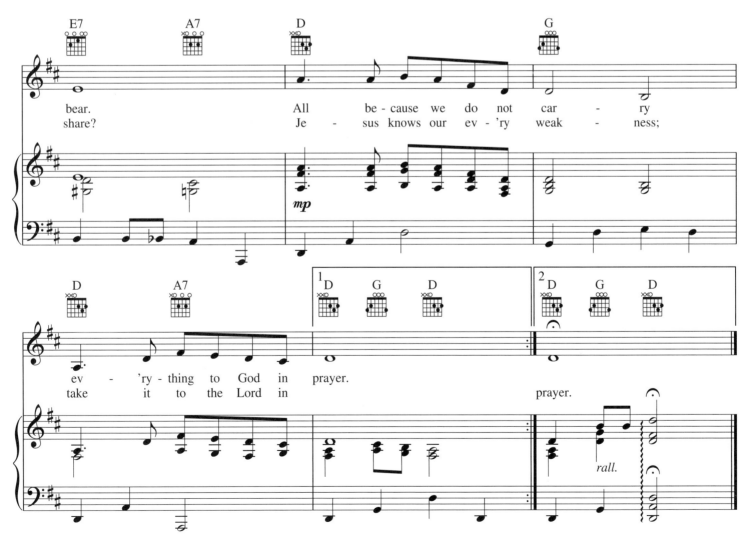

STANDING ON THE PROMISES

Words and Music by
R. KELSO CARTER

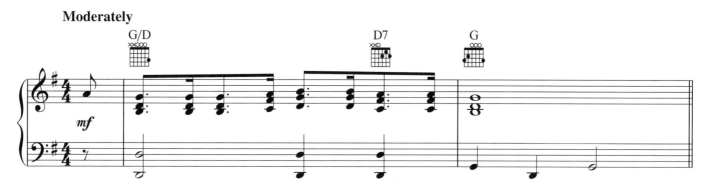

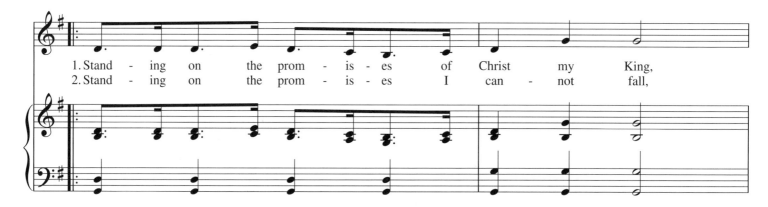

1. Stand - ing on the prom - is - es of Christ my King,
2. Stand - ing on the prom - is - es I can - not fall,

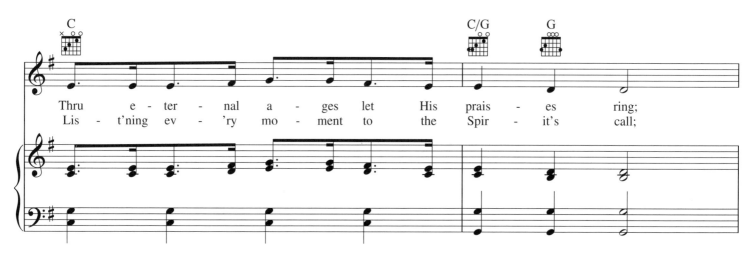

Thru e - ter - nal a - ges let His prais - es ring;
Lis - t'ning ev - 'ry mo - ment to the Spir - it's call;

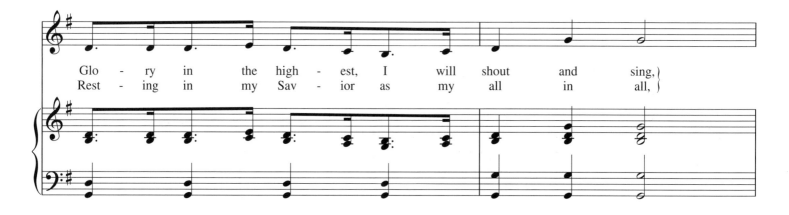

Glo - ry in the high - est, I will shout and sing,
Rest - ing in my Sav - ior as my all in all,

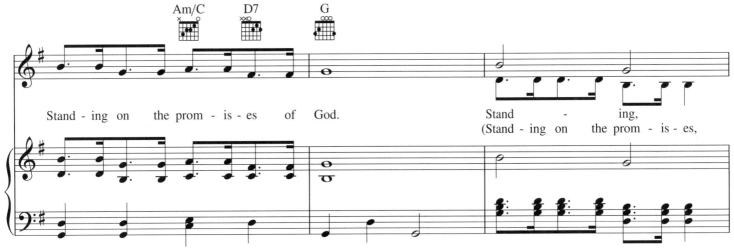

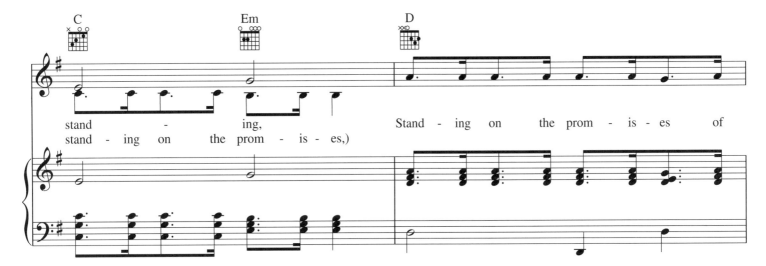

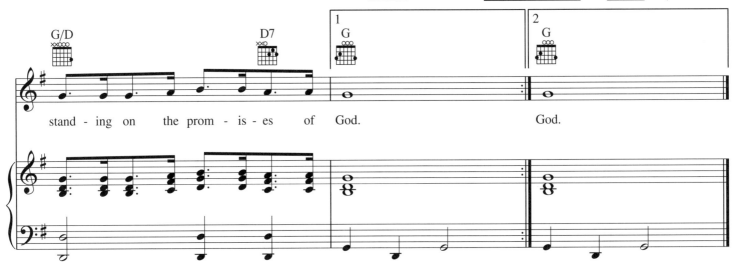

TURN YOUR EYES UPON JESUS

Words and Music by
HELEN H. LEMMEL

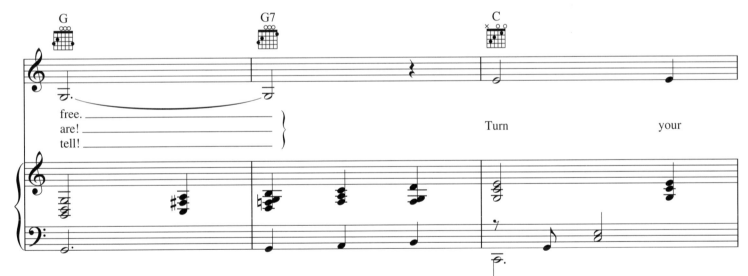

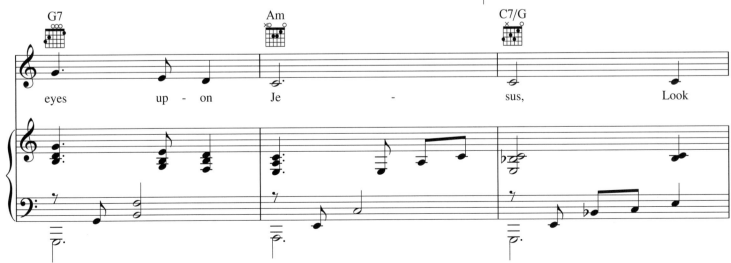

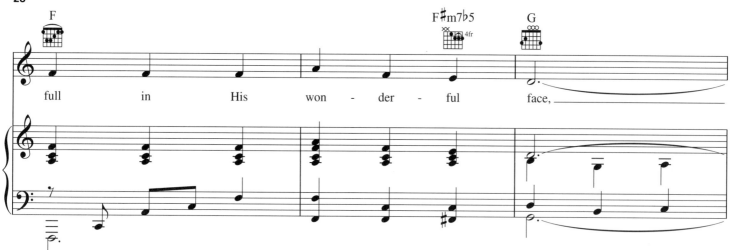

full in His won-der-ful face, ___

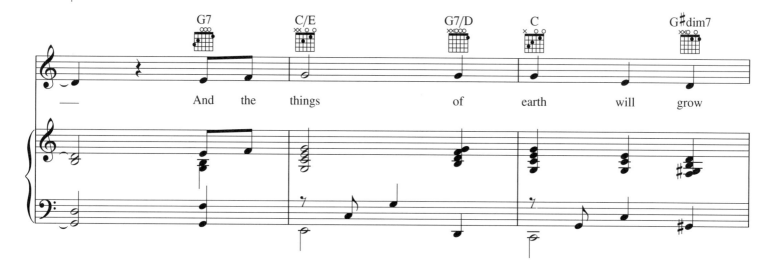

___ And the things of earth will grow

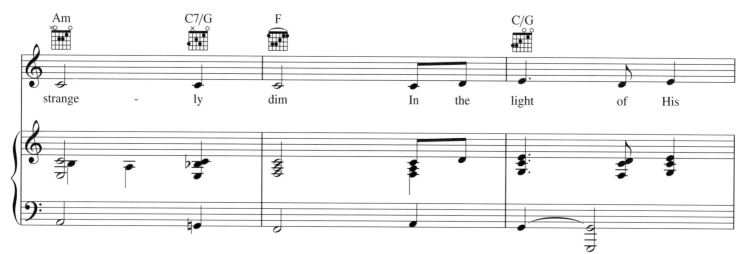

strange-ly dim In the light of His

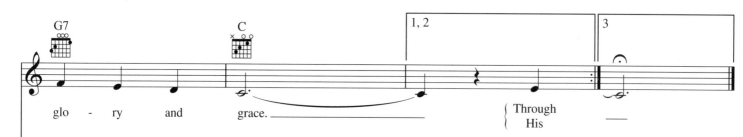

glo-ry and grace. ___ { Through His

LEANING ON THE EVERLASTING ARMS

Words by ELISHA A. HOFFMAN
Music by ANTHONY J. SHOWALTER

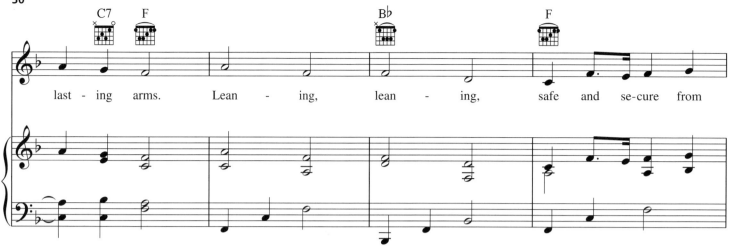

last - ing arms. Lean - ing, lean - ing, safe and se-cure from

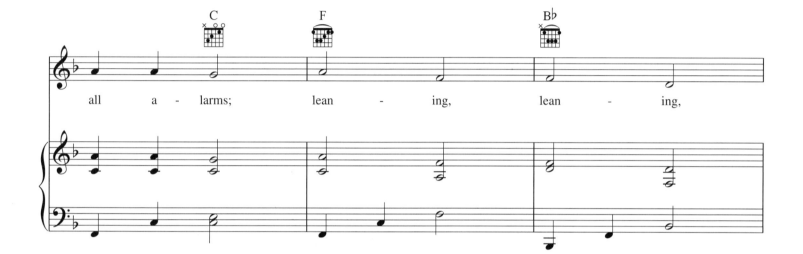

all a - larms; lean - ing, lean - ing,

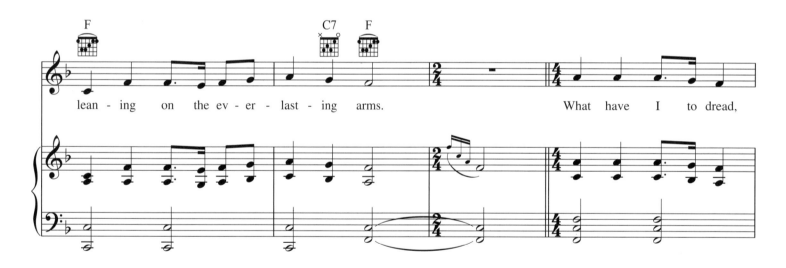

lean - ing on the ev - er - last - ing arms. What have I to dread,

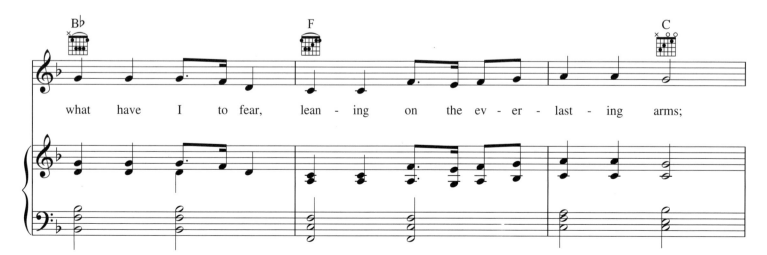

what have I to fear, lean - ing on the ev - er - last - ing arms;

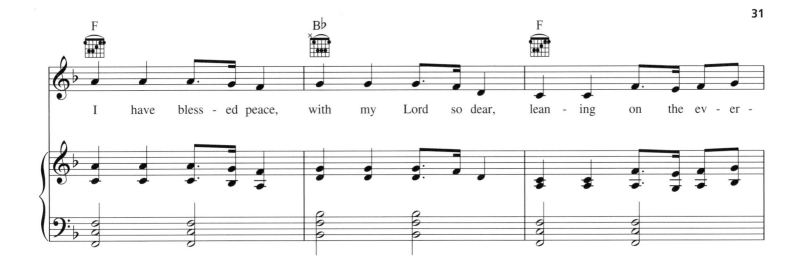

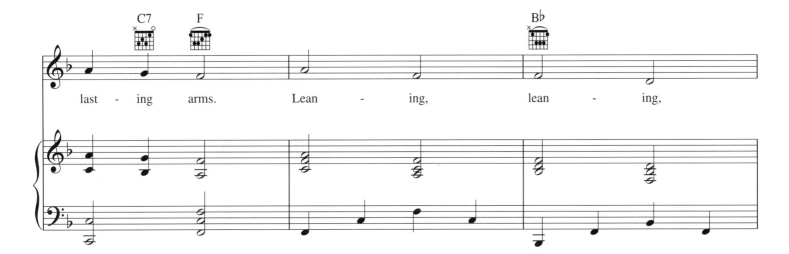

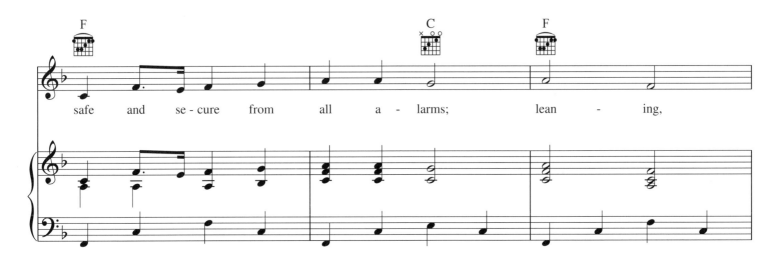

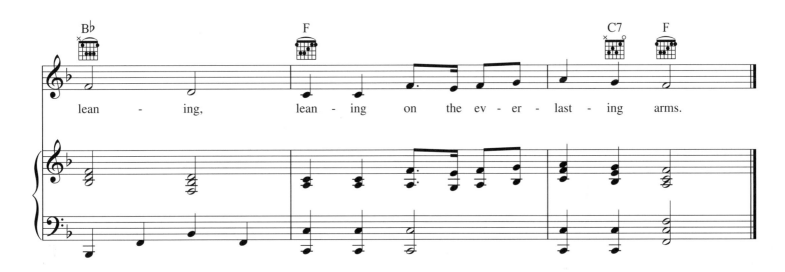

HOW GREAT THOU ART

Words and Music by
STUART K. HINE

G
C
G
played, ___ Then sings my soul, my Sav - ior God to Thee, ___ How great Thou
art; ___
D7
G
C
art, ___ how great Thou art! ___ Then sings my soul, my Sav - ior God to
G
Am
D7
1
G
D7
2
G
Thee; ___ How great Thou art, ___ how great Thou art! ___ When Christ shall art!

I WANT TO STROLL OVER HEAVEN WITH YOU

Words and Music by
J.B. LEMLEY

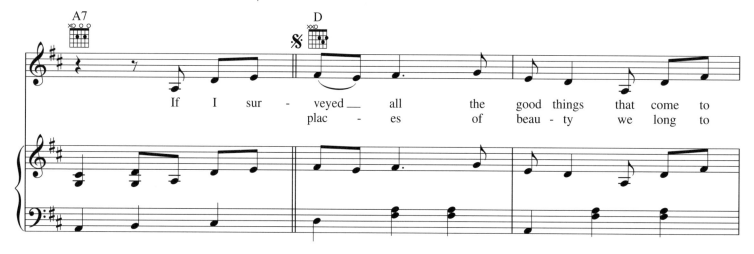

If I sur- veyed ___ all the good things that come to
plac- es of beau- ty we long to

me from a- bove, ___ if I count ___ all the
see here be- low, ___ but time and treas- ures the have

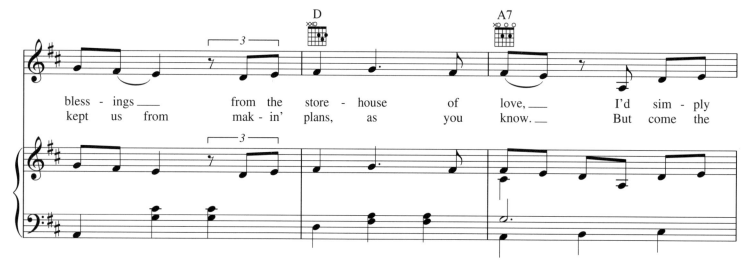

bless- ings ___ from the store- house of love, ___ I'd sim- ply
kept us from mak- in' plans, as you know. ___ But come the

ask ___ for a fa - vor of Him be - yond mor - tal
morn - ing of the rap - ture, to - geth - er we'll stand a -

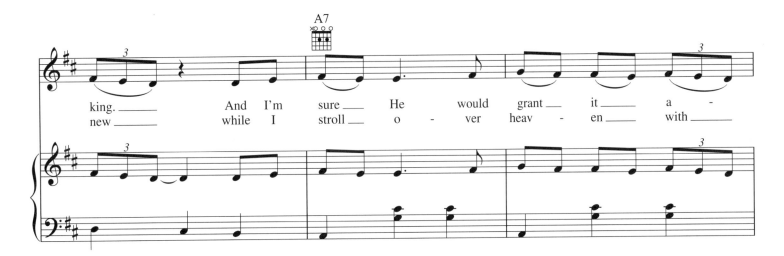

king. ___ And I'm sure ___ He would grant ___ it ___ a -
new ___ while I stroll ___ o - ver heav - en ___ with ___

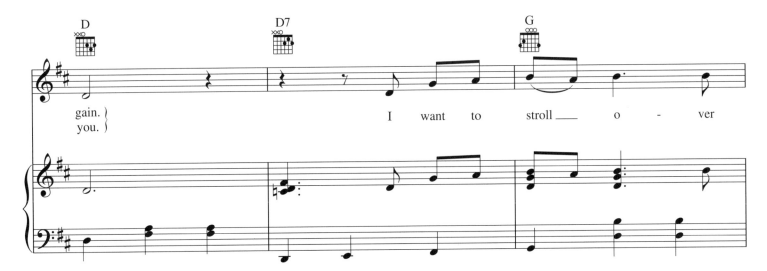

gain. }
you.   } I want to stroll ___ o - ver

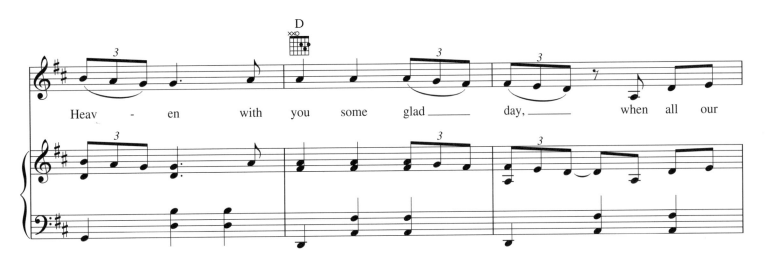

Heav - en with you some glad ___ day, ___ when all our

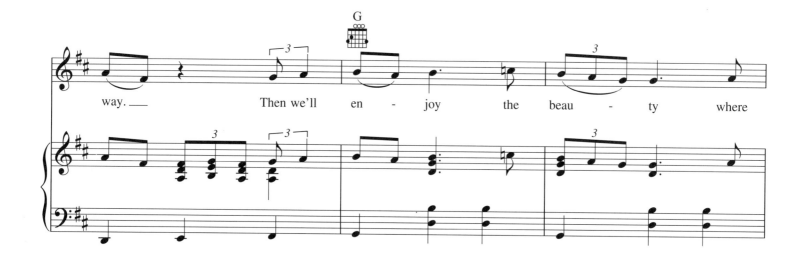

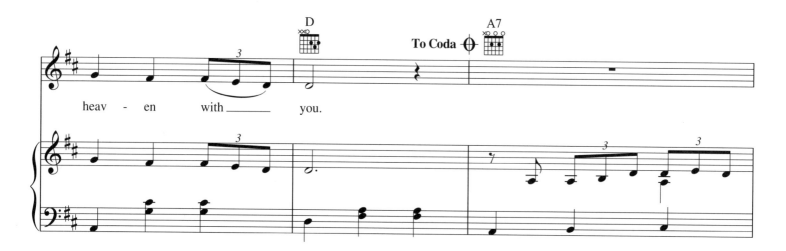

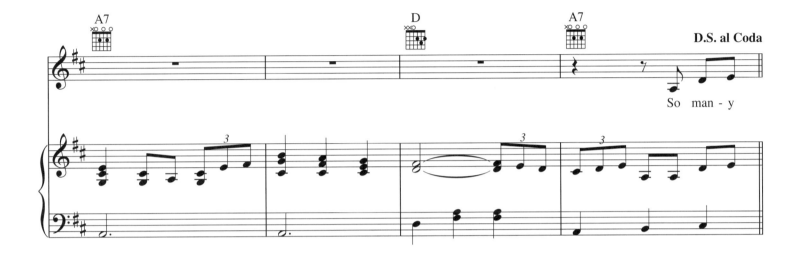

So man - y

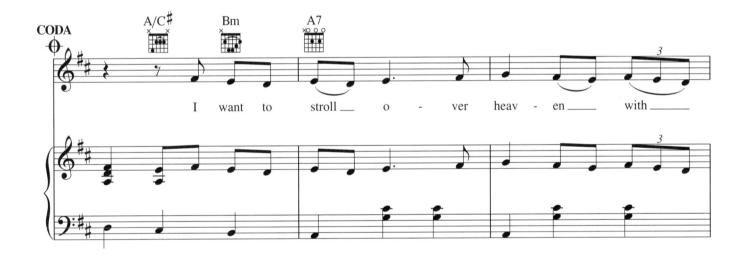

I want to stroll ___ o - ver heav - en ___ with ___

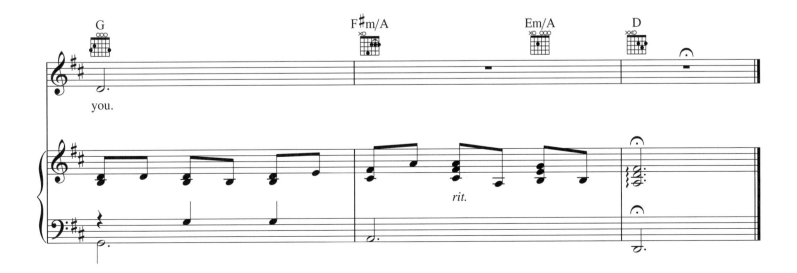

you.

rit.

THE OLD RUGGED CROSS

By REV. GEORGE BENNARD

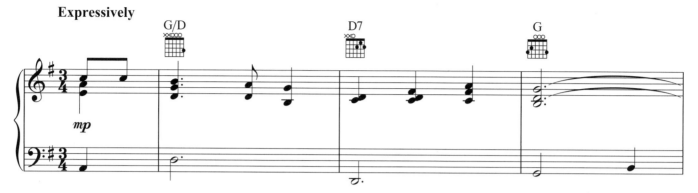

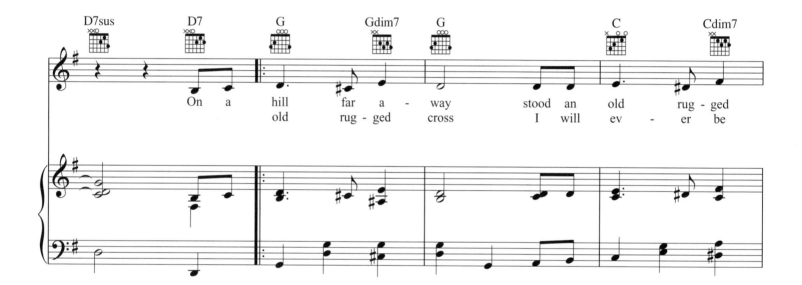

On a hill far a - way stood an old rug - ged
old rug - ged cross I will ev - er be

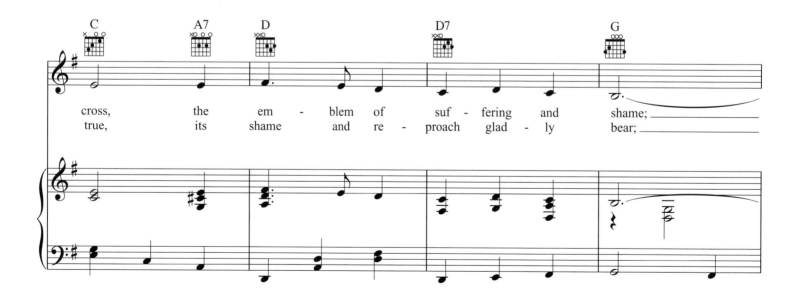

cross, the em - blem of suf - fering and shame;
true, its shame and re - proach glad - ly bear;

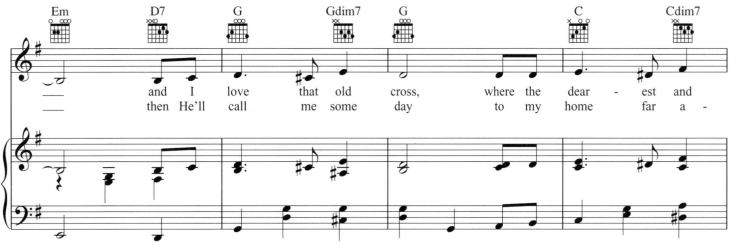

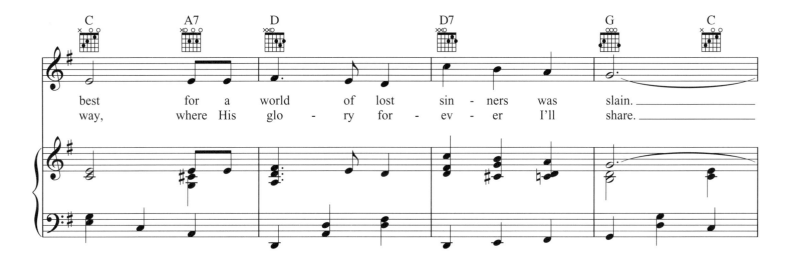

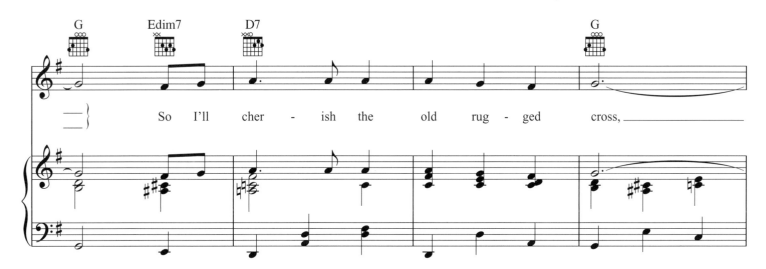

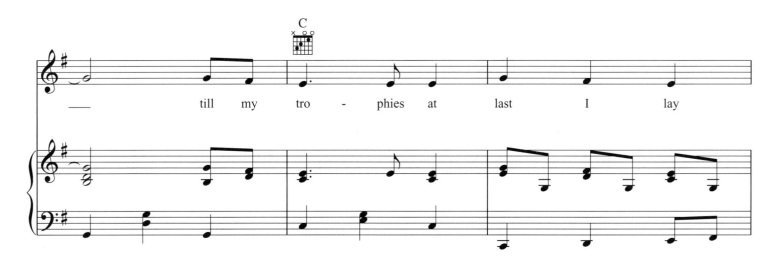

down; _____ I will cling to the old rug - ged

cross, _____ and ex - change it some day for a

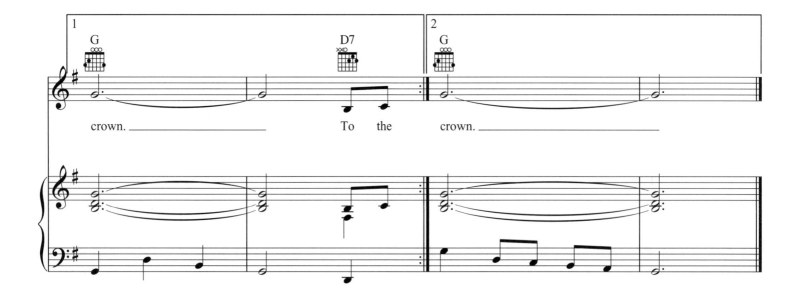

crown. _____ To the crown. _____